St. Mary's RC Primary

2387

ST. MARY'S R.C.
PRIMARY SCHOOL
EAST ROW W10 5AW
TEL: 0181-969 0321 - 3710
FAX: 0181 964 - 3122

The School Outing

Diana Bentley
Reading Consultant
University of Reading

Photographs by
Tim Woodcock

My School

The Class Teacher
The Dinner Ladies
The Lollipop Man
The Road Safety Officer
The School Caretaker
The School Fête
The School Outing
The School Secretary

First published in 1988 by
Wayland (Publishers) Limited
61 Western Road, Hove
East Sussex, BN3 1JD, England

© Copyright 1988 Wayland (Publishers) Limited

British Library Cataloguing in Publication Data
Bentley, Diana
    The school outing. – (My school).
    1. Schools – Juvenile literature
    I. Title   II. Series
    371   LA132
ISBN 1–85210–273–X

Phototypeset by
Kalligraphics Limited
Redhill, Surrey
Printed and bound by
Casterman S.A., Belgium

Contents

Today we are going to visit a farm	8
The farmer meets us	10
We go to see the cows	12
We meet a friendly calf and a horse	14
There are piglets and goats too	16
At lunchtime we have a picnic	18
After lunch we do some work	20
We race each other down the hill	22
We stroke the friendly horse	24
Time to go home	26
Glossary	28
Books to read	29
Index	30

All the words that appear in **bold** are explained in the glossary on page 28.

Hello. Today we are going to visit a farm.

Today we are going on an outing to a farm in Essex. For many of us it is our first visit to a farm. It is very exciting. A coach picks us up from school. Can you see Edward boarding the coach? The coach takes us to the farm.

The farmer meets us. He takes us to see the animals.

The farmer comes to meet us. He looks after the farm. He is going to take us to see the animals. In the farmyard we see an old **tractor**. It is not used any more. We have great fun playing on it. Look at the back wheels. They are very big.

We go to see the cows in the barn.

We go to see the cows in the barn. The farmer says, 'Mind the big cow, she looks fierce!'. Inside the barn there is a Highland cow. She has long brown hair and big horns. We don't like to get too close because she looks very grumpy.

We meet a friendly calf and an old horse.

Ben and Elliot find a calf. She is very friendly and lets us stroke her long hair. We try to give her some **straw** to eat. Some of us find a big horse. People used to ride this horse, but now she is too old for riding. We stroke her too.

There are piglets and a goat in the barn.

We see some piglets sleeping on the straw. They all have bright pink ears. Our teacher shows us a goat. It licks our teacher's fingers. Goats give us milk. Have you ever drunk goats' milk?

At lunchtime we have a picnic in the field.

At lunchtime we all sit down in the field. We are all very hungry. We have brought a picnic with us. We eat sandwiches and crisps. Farhad is giving a crisp to the black and white cat. But the cat doesn't like it. Digby is enjoying his **yoghurt**.

After lunch we do some work.

After lunch we talk about what we have seen on the farm. Edward lies on his tummy and draw the animals he has seen. Our teacher talks to us about some of the **crops** grown on the farm. Some farms grow mainly crops and some farms have animals. Our teacher has some **wheat** in her hand. Wheat is used to make bread.

We race each other down the hill to see more animals.

There are more cows and horses in fields at the bottom of the hill. We race each other down the hill. There is a cow with long horns. She looks fierce. But we are safe on this side of the fence.

We stroke the friendly brown horse.

We meet a friendly brown horse. She lifts her head over the fence. She has soft hair and a long **mane**. We all try to stroke her. The horse is eating the grass. If we stand on the fence we can just reach the horse.

Time to go home. We all walk back to the coach.

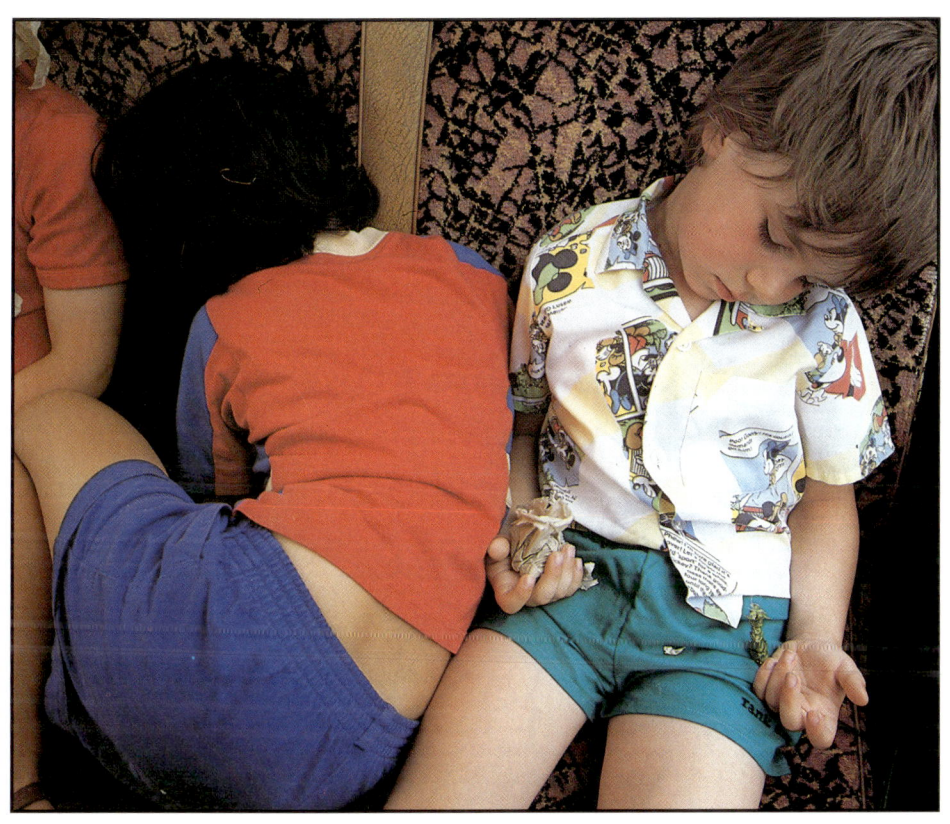

Now our visit to the farm is over. We have a long walk back to the coach. It has been an exciting day. But now we are all very tired. On the journey home Harry and his friend fall asleep. They sleep all the way home. Perhaps they are dreaming about the animals.

Glossary

Crops A general name for the things that grow on a farm, such as wheat, fruit and vegetables.

Mane The long hair that grows on the neck of some animals, such as horses.

Straw Dried grass that has been stored by the farmer. It is used as bedding for the animals.

Tractor A vehicle used by the farmer to pull heavy loads.

Wheat A kind of grass. We use its grain to make bread.

Yoghurt A dessert made of thickened milk, often with a fruit flavour.

Acknowledgement

The author and publishers would like to thank the head teacher, staff and pupils of Rhodes Avenue Infant School, Wood Green, London.

Books to read

A Day with a Farmer by Allan and Christine Haddrell (Wayland, 1980)
Autumn on the Farm by Peggy Heeks and Ralph Whitlock (Wayland, 1985)
Let's Go to the Farm by Roland Lenga (Franklin Watts, 1980)
Spring on the Farm by Peggy Heeks and Ralph Whitlock (Wayland, 1985)
Summer on the Farm by Peggy Heeks and Ralph Whitlock (Wayland, 1985)
The Farmer by M Graham-Cameron (Dinosaur Publications, 1980)
The Farmer by Ann Stewart (Hamish Hamilton, 1983)
Winter on the Farm by Peggy Heeks and Ralph Whitlock (Wayland, 1985)

Index

animals 10, 11, 21, 22, 27

barn 12

calf 15
cat 18
coach 8, 26, 27
cow 12, 22
crops 21, 28

farmer 10, 11
farmyard 11

goat 16

horse 15, 25

milk 16

picnic 18
piglets 16

straw 15, 28

tractor 11, 28

wheat 21, 28